PERFECT
PIZZA
AT HOME

Also in This Series

The Artisanal Kitchen: Perfect Pasta

The Artisanal Kitchen: Vegetables the Italian Way

THE ARTISANAL KITCHEN

PERFECT
PIZZA
AT HOME

FROM THE ESSENTIAL DOUGH TO
THE TASTIEST TOPPINGS

ANDREW FEINBERG & FRANCINE STEPHENS
OF FRANNY'S RESTAURANT

WITH MELISSA CLARK

ARTISAN ■ NEW YORK

Contents

Introduction

Pizza just might be the perfect food, a magical substance that pleases most people, of most ages, most of the time. People never seem to tire of pizza. My husband, Andrew, and I have been eating at our restaurant, Franny's, as a couple and then as a family, many times a week for the several years we've been open. And I can honestly say that I have never gotten sick of pizza. Neither have our regulars. Whether it's a quick solo bite at the bar on the way home from work, a date-night feast, or a weekend lunch with out-of-town guests, a meal at Franny's always (or nearly always) seems to include at least one pizza.

That was part of the plan when we opened. We wanted to create a place where our friends could come every night— where people would crave the food and want to come back again and again. So far, so good. And once we came up with the idea of opening a pizza restaurant, it seemed obvious.

The concept was a given—but getting the pizza itself right was another matter. Other than a love of pizza and our trips to Italy, we didn't have a lot to go on. When we opened Franny's, we were at the forefront of a pizza renaissance. While there are now artisanal, wood-fired, brick-oven pizza restaurants in San Francisco, Los Angeles, Seattle, Chicago . . . virtually everywhere, when we opened, there were only a handful. We love that we caught this new-style pizza wave right at the beginning.

Before we opened in our original space, we hired a third-generation brick-oven builder from Naples to build our hulking brick oven, and then we got to work. When Andrew looks back on the early days of Franny's, he is genuinely appalled: we opened a restaurant based on a food that we didn't really know how to cook. (Chalk it up to youthful naïveté and optimism.) For the first few weeks after we opened, Andrew rolled out the pizza dough with a rolling pin, and the result was all wrong; the rolled-out crusts were crackery and dry. And he cooked the tomato sauce on the stove, as you would for pasta, which stripped it of all its complexity and vibrancy.

But one of the many things I love about Andrew is that he is always researching, reading books, tweaking, experimenting, and not resting until a dish is right. He and the other folks in the kitchen taught each other how to cook pizza, handing knowledge back and forth. The recipes and techniques in this book, all of which are based on traditional Neapolitan-style pizza, represent years of experience.

The pizza made in Naples is taken so seriously in Italy that some pizzas have been designated with governmental protection. To be called a *pizza Margherita* in Italy, a pizza has to meet strict guidelines that govern everything from the type of flour used in the dough to the temperature at which it is baked. True Neapolitan-style pizza is soft throughout (the dough is tender and chewy), and there's a restrained amount of cheese and sauce (both of very high quality). Overall, pizza in Naples is a subtler affair than pizza in America. While Andrew and I respect and admire authentic Neapolitan pizza, and have learned so much from it, we've ultimately gone our own way. Our pizza is a little bit different from anything you'd find in Naples, or anywhere else in this country, for that matter.

Of course, the foundation of any pizza is the dough. Ours is yeasty and deeply flavorful, with just the right balance of crispness and chewiness. Stretching the pizza out by hand means it puffs spectacularly in the hot oven and forms a few large bubbles around the edges, which take on a crackling black char. The key to the flavor and texture is using a small amount of yeast and letting the dough rise slowly in the fridge, where it has a chance to develop complexity and nuance. We strongly advise against using instant yeast to hurry things along. Patience, we've learned, is part and parcel of making great pizza.

Then there's the sauce. It turns out that the easiest sauce is in fact the best. Taking our cue from Naples, we puree high-quality canned San Marzano tomatoes, then season them aggressively. That's all you need for a bright, lush sauce, and it couldn't be simpler to do.

When it comes to the toppings, there's plenty of room for creativity. But whatever you choose to put on your pizza, use a light hand. You want balance: balance between the sauce and the dough, between the cheese and the anchovy, and so on. Some of our pizza toppings are as traditional as can be (see our version of a Margherita, page 55), while others are purely of our own invention (for example, the Tomato, Provolone Piccante, and Roasted Onion Pizza, page 59). Some, of course, are decidedly seasonal (like our Flowering Broccoli Pizza, page 23), in keeping with our overall philosophy.

Whatever the ingredients we put on our pizzas, we make sure they are superb. We buy the best cheeses we can find, and they're worth every penny. For most of our pizzas, that means buffalo mozzarella, which adds a distinct creamy complexity and depth of flavor. For more elaborate pizzas with other meats, you can use either buffalo mozzarella or a good-quality fresh cow's-milk mozzarella. We've done it both ways, and while we've ultimately come to prefer the more pronounced taste of the buffalo, the buttery milkiness of the cow's-milk cheese next to the pungency of sausage or meatballs is also marvelous. As long as the cheese you buy is fresh and well made, whichever mozzarella you choose will be delicious.

Pizza is a great blank canvas for whatever you love, so feel free to change things up to suit your taste. Skip the capers if you're not a fan, or pile them on if you are. Or swap out roasted eggplant for roasted peppers or add olives or anchovies to the Tomato, Garlic, Oregano, and Extra-Virgin Olive Oil Pizza (page 85). Start out with a simple pizza and build from there—if you like onions and sausage together, by all means put them both on your pizza. If you like things spicy, add a generous amount of chili flakes. That said, all of the recipes in this book are perfectly calibrated, so we do recommend making them as written at least once—especially the Clam, Chili, and Parsley Pizza (page 51). Follow the recipe to the letter, and you'll be bowled over by its gorgeous, briny perfection.

For baking pizza at home, we came up with a method using a conventional oven that results in a close approximation of the puffed, charred pizzas you get from a wood-fired brick oven (though without the wood-smoke flavor). You do need a pizza stone. If you don't have one, buy the thickest, sturdiest one you can find. Preheat the stone in a 500°F oven for an hour. When you slide in your pizza, the fierce heat from the stone will immediately start baking the bottom crust. Then, after 3 minutes, turn off the oven and turn on the broiler, which will blister the top of the pizza, so your pizza is basically cooked from both top and bottom.

If your oven has a separate broiler, you can still use this technique, but it will require an extra step. After cooking the pizza on the stone in the oven, preheat the broiler. Use tongs to move the half-baked pizza onto a baking sheet and run it under the broiler until the top of the pizza browns, about a minute or two. The results will be just as good.

All of the recipes in this book make four individual pizzas. At the restaurant, it's rare for a table of four to order, say, four sausage pizzas or four white pizzas. People order an array of choices, since pizza is ideal for sharing (another part of what makes it so appealing). At home, you could do the same thing and improvise four different pizzas. Don't feel hemmed in. Make the dough and then top each round individually and separately.

For example, you could start out with an EVOO pizza (see page 21), then move on to a Flowering Broccoli Pizza (page 23). Wrap things up with a hearty Tomato, Mozzarella, and Sausage Pizza (page 61) and a creamy Buffalo Mozzarella, Ricotta, Garlic, Oregano, and Hot Pepper Pizza (page 41) as the "cheese course." Get the kids involved in the process, letting them help top the pizza. It's just the kind of cooking that kids love to be a part of. And there's no need to fret about timing. Share each pizza as you make it, and no one will go hungry waiting. (If you're lucky enough to have a dual-oven setup in your home kitchen, buy two pizza stones and make two pizzas at once!)

Although making pizza does take some advance preparation, with a little planning and practice, your dinner can take shape pretty quickly. Freeze a bunch of individually portioned sauces and dough balls, then put them in the fridge to defrost before you start your day. You'll have fresh homemade pizza fixings at the ready when you get home. Pizza at home can satisfy an urgent craving, or it can be the centerpiece of a convivial dinner with good friends.

—Francine Stephens

Franny's Pizza Dough

We opened a pizza place with a lot to learn about making pizza. Our first pizzas were wildly inconsistent; we were honestly amazed that anyone who ate one ever came back. We knew what we were looking for: a chewy, flavorful thin crust, burnished all over from the oven and crisp on the bottom, with a few of those delicious bubbles that rise and brown here and there on a great pizza.

Andrew read everything he could about the science of yeast doughs, and he experimented with the amount of yeast, the amount and protein content of the flour, the amount of salt, the amount of kneading, and the rising time. The winning formula (which took years to find) is actually very easy. We use the bare minimum of yeast. We let the dough proof (aka rise) slowly, at least overnight, in the fridge, so it becomes way more flavorful than it would rising faster at a warmer temperature, and the gluten develops perfectly—the secret to a chewy, gorgeous crust. Then, after the dough is brought back to room temperature, it's ready to be stretched out (do not roll it!). This method means you'll want to start making your pizza at least 24 hours, and preferably 48 hours, ahead.

While it's not something we do at Franny's, we discovered that this dough freezes really well. If you want to freeze it, after shaping the dough into balls, tightly wrap each ball individually in plastic wrap, place in a resealable freezer bag, and freeze (for up to 3 months). Defrost overnight, or for at least 12 hours, in the refrigerator, or for 2 to 4 hours at room temperature, before using. Feel free to double this recipe if you are feeding a crowd. | **MAKES 2 POUNDS, ENOUGH FOR FOUR 12-INCH PIZZAS**

CONTINUED

2 packed teaspoons fresh yeast (10 grams) or 1½ teaspoons active dry yeast

1¾ cups cold water
4½ cups all-purpose flour
2 teaspoons kosher salt

If using fresh yeast, mix the water and yeast together in the bowl of a stand mixer until the yeast is dissolved. If using active dry yeast, mix the water and yeast in the bowl and let sit until the yeast is foamy, about 5 minutes.

Using the dough hook, beat in the flour and salt and mix until a smooth, slightly elastic dough forms, 2 to 3 minutes; do not knead. Place the dough in an oiled bowl, turn the dough to coat, cover loosely with plastic, and refrigerate for at least 24 hours, and up to 48 hours, to proof. (At Franny's we let it proof for 48 hours, at which point we feel the dough has the optimal texture and flavor, but you've got some leeway at home.)

When you are ready to make the pizza, divide the dough into 4 equal pieces. Shape each piece by using the palm of your hand to rotate the dough clockwise until a tight, compact ball has formed. Turn the dough over. Working from the outside in, pinch and twist the edges of the dough into the center to make a very tight ball. Put the dough on a baking sheet and return to the refrigerator to rest for at least 4 hours, and up to 12 hours.

When you are ready to make the pizzas, remove the dough from the refrigerator and let it sit at room temperature for at least 30 minutes (take the dough out of the fridge while you preheat the pizza stone). You can let it sit out longer, as long as it doesn't get too soft and floppy, which would make it difficult to shape; soft dough is also more likely to stick to the baking sheet or pizza peel, making it harder to slide onto the stone. If the dough gets too soft, stick it back in the fridge for 10 minutes or so to give it a chance to firm up. Shape and top as directed in the individual pizza recipes.

Franny's Pizza Sauce

This pizza sauce is so simple it's almost shocking: all you do is blend uncooked canned tomatoes with a good dose of salt and pepper. Then you spoon it onto the unbaked crust, and the high heat of the oven cooks the sauce just enough to accentuate the tomato flavor and thicken it—no need to simmer it on the stove. And keeping the ingredients to a bare minimum means you'll be able to taste the crust and other toppings without the sauce dominating the pizza.

As far as the texture goes, it's really up to you, but we like to leave some small chunks in there (about the size of a pea)—the sauce shouldn't be completely chunky, but we also don't want it entirely smooth. If you've got plenty of room in your freezer, make two or even three batches. Freeze in plastic bags, in individual pizza-sized portions (about 3 tablespoons per pizza), and it will defrost in a flash and be ready for you when you need it. | **MAKES ABOUT 2½ CUPS**

One 28-ounce can whole
  San Marzano tomatoes,
  drained

½ teaspoon kosher salt, or
  more to taste
¼ teaspoon freshly cracked
  black pepper

Using a food mill fitted with the large-holed disk, or a food processor, puree the tomatoes until slightly coarse and loose, not completely smooth. Season with the salt and pepper.

CONTINUED

Note: Most Italian cooking experts agree that San Marzanos are the best sauce tomatoes in the world. Their flesh is dense, there are fewer seeds, and their strong, sweet flavor is balanced with acidity. San Marzano tomatoes have been designated as the only tomatoes that can be used for true Neapolitan pizza—only tomatoes grown in the San Marzano region from seeds dating back to the original cultivar, and according to strict standards, can receive the Denominazione d'Origine Protetta (DOP) label. If you do not see the prominently displayed DOP label, you are not getting certified San Marzanos. At the restaurant, we usually use the Strianese brand, but there are many others widely available, such as Cento, La Valle, and Caluccio—just look for the DOP label and you'll know you're getting an authentic product. If you can't find DOP San Marzanos, make sure you substitute another tomato with a good balance of sweetness and acidity.

Pizza Techniques

1. Lightly flour an upside-down baking sheet or a pizza peel. You'll use this to transfer the dough onto your pizza stone.

2. Place a dough ball on a lightly floured work surface. Dust the top of the dough with additional flour, and use your fingertips to flatten the dough into a round. Forming the dough into nice even rounds takes practice, but don't worry—even if your dough comes out lopsided and a little funny-looking, the pizza will still taste great.

3. Holding the dough in front of you as you would hold a steering wheel (with hands positioned at ten o'clock and two o'clock), rotate the dough several times, stretching it as you do so. Let the weight of the dough help stretch it. Then move your fists about 6 inches apart and place the dough over your knuckles. Toss the dough in a circle over your knuckles, using your fists to stretch the dough. Try to maintain as even a thickness as possible, with the edges of the dough slightly thicker. Continue until you have a 12-inch round.

4. Carefully set the dough on the floured baking sheet or pizza peel. Patch any tears or holes in the dough.

5. Use a light touch when topping the dough. You need fewer ingredients and less of them than you might think. You want to be able to taste the charred pizza crust itself, not just the toppings.

6. Before sliding the pizza onto the pizza stone, give the baking sheet (or peel) a shake to make sure the pizza isn't sticking anywhere. If it is, lift up the stuck part and sprinkle more flour underneath it. The pizza needs to easily slide from baking sheet to stone.

7. If you don't have a pizza peel, use tongs to remove the pizza from the oven and transfer to a platter or a cutting board.

8. As a finishing touch to the pizza, a sprinkling of sea salt, a drizzle of olive oil, and often a handful of grated Parmigiano-Reggiano or Grana Padano after the pizza is baked adds yet another layer of flavor and texture.

Extra-Virgin Olive Oil and Sea Salt Pizza

On one of our early trips to Italy, we went into a Roman restaurant and ordered a *pizza bianca*, anticipating one of the cheesy white pizzas we always got in New York. When it arrived, we were confused—it looked like focaccia, without any cheese at all, just a smattering of herbs and a sheen of olive oil. But, as so often happens in Italy, the first bite took away all our doubts. The pizza was perfect in its simplicity, and we came straight home to replicate it.

Very early in the restaurant's tenure, we made this pizza with fresh rosemary and thin slivers of garlic baked on top. While that version is totally delicious, we stripped it down even further and finish the pizza with just a sprinkle of big, crunchy flakes of sea salt.

Of all the pizzas at Franny's, this is the one that lets you taste the bare elements the most. There's no missing the satisfying char that develops, or the slight tang of the yeast. And it's a great showcase for super-high-quality olive oil. At the restaurant, this pizza is a true test for any new cook—getting one out of a 900°F wood-fired oven at the right time can be tricky. Fortunately for you, this pizza is actually much easier to make at home. And it's a great way to start off your meal. | **MAKES FOUR 12-INCH PIZZAS, SERVING 4 TO 6**

CONTINUED

Franny's Pizza Dough (page 13)
All-purpose flour

¼ cup extra-virgin olive oil, plus
   more for drizzling
Sea salt

Preheat the oven to 500°F, with a pizza stone on a rack in the top third of the oven. Let heat for 1 hour. Remove the pizza dough from the refrigerator at least 30 minutes before baking.

Turn a large baking sheet upside down, or use a pizza peel. Dust the surface with flour. Form one piece of the dough into a 12-inch round (see page 18) and set it on the baking sheet or peel.

Working quickly, drizzle the dough with 1 tablespoon of the olive oil.

Jiggle the pizza gently on the pan (or peel) to make sure it is not sticking (if it is, loosen it and sprinkle a little more flour under the area where it stuck). Slide the pizza onto the hot stone, making sure to start at the stone's back end so that the entire pizza will fit on it.

Cook the pizza for 3 minutes. Turn on the broiler. Broil the pizza until golden, crisp, and a bit blistery and charred in places, 2 to 4 minutes (watch it carefully to see that it does not burn). If you don't have a peel, use tongs to slide the pizza onto a large platter. Finish with a drizzling of olive oil and a generous sprinkling of sea salt.

Repeat with the remaining dough and toppings.

Note: Because this pizza's only topping is the olive oil, you need to keep a closer eye on it than you do with the other pizzas. Without the weight and moisture of sauce and/or cheese, bubbles tend to form, so the dough can rise and then char fairly quickly. If you see big bubbles rising, just give them a few bangs with the handle of a wooden spoon or puncture them with a paring knife.

Flowering Broccoli Pizza

One of our favorite vendors at Brooklyn's Grand Army Plaza Greenmarket is Kira Kinney's Evolutionary Organics. Kira grows overwintered greens that blossom into sweet little sprouts by about April. Flowering kale, flowering broccoli, even flowering bok choy—topped with yellow and white buds, these plants are almost like an edible bouquet of wildflowers, a welcome sight after a long winter.

Chef John Adler came up with this simple, vibrant pizza as a great way to get some greens on the menu at a time when they are in short supply. There's no tomato sauce, because the pizza doesn't need it—the focus is all on the interplay among the broccoli leaves, stems, and flowers. Some of the leaves will char a touch (delicious), and the stems roast just enough to take on a complex sweetness. Finished with some sharp Pecorino Romano and a squeeze of lemon, this pizza has swayed many a traditionalist at the restaurant. Regular broccoli rabe would work fine here too. Just pull the florets apart into small pieces and slice the stems into ¼-inch-thick slivers. | **MAKES FOUR 12-INCH PIZZAS, SERVING 4 TO 6**

Franny's Pizza Dough (page 13)

8 ounces flowering greens,
  such as broccoli rabe

All-purpose flour

4 small garlic cloves, shaved
  into paper-thin slices with
  a knife or a mandoline

Chili flakes

4 ounces Parmigiano-Reggiano
  or Grana Padano, finely
  grated (about 1 cup)

¼ cup extra-virgin olive oil, plus
  more for drizzling

2 ounces Pecorino Romano,
  finely grated (about ½ cup)

2 lemons, halved

CONTINUED

Preheat the oven to 500°F, with a pizza stone on a rack in the top third of the oven. Let heat for 1 hour. Remove the pizza dough from the refrigerator at least 30 minutes before baking.

Coarsely chop the tops of the flowering greens. Trim away any woody stem ends and cut the remaining stems into halves or quarters (¼ inch thick is good; you should have about 4 cups greens and stems total).

Turn a large baking sheet upside down, or use a pizza peel. Dust the surface with flour. Form one piece of the dough into a 12-inch round (see page 18) and set it on the baking sheet or peel.

Working quickly, scatter the dough with one-fourth of the garlic and a pinch of chili flakes followed by one-fourth of the greens. Sprinkle with one-fourth of the Parmigiano-Reggiano and drizzle with 1 tablespoon of the olive oil.

Jiggle the pizza gently on the pan (or peel) to make sure it is not sticking (if it is, loosen it and sprinkle a little more flour under the area where it stuck). Slide the pizza onto the hot stone, making sure to start at the stone's back end so that the entire pizza will fit on it.

Cook the pizza for 3 minutes. Turn on the broiler. Broil the pizza until golden, crisp, and a bit blistery and charred in places, 2 to 4 minutes (watch it carefully to see that it does not burn). If you don't have a peel, use tongs to slide the pizza onto a large platter. Drizzle with more olive oil, sprinkle with one-fourth of the Pecorino Romano, and squeeze the juice of ½ lemon over the top.

Repeat with the remaining dough and toppings.

Asparagus, Garlic, Chili, and Mozzarella Pizza

Asparagus has a short season in many parts of the country; in New York, it's really only about a month long. So we try to use it as much as possible during that time. At home, Andrew likes to roast the spears until they brown and soften and turn very sweet. Then he mixes them with some Calabrian chili for a fiery contrast and a squeeze of lemon for acidity. This is the same concept, transferred to a pizza. This recipe is one of Franny's newer pizzas, and it quickly became a favorite. We all look forward to it every spring. | **MAKES FOUR 12-INCH PIZZAS, SERVING 4 TO 6**

Franny's Pizza Dough (page 13)
1½ pounds asparagus
(about 1½ bunches), **trimmed**
3 tablespoons extra-virgin olive
oil, plus more for drizzling
¼ teaspoon kosher salt
All-purpose flour
1 teaspoon Calabrian chili paste
(see Note), **or to taste**
4 large garlic cloves, shaved
into paper-thin slices with
a knife or a mandoline

10 ounces fresh cow's-milk
mozzarella, pulled into
large bite-sized pieces
(about 1½ cups)
2 ounces Grana Padano,
finely grated (about ½ cup),
plus more for sprinkling
Juice of 2 lemons, or to taste
Sea salt

Preheat the oven to 500°F, with a pizza stone on a rack in the top third of the oven. Let heat for 1 hour. Remove the pizza dough from the refrigerator at least 30 minutes before baking.

Meanwhile, once the oven has preheated (while the pizza stone continues to heat), toss the asparagus with the olive oil and salt. Spread on a large rimmed baking sheet and roast, tossing the asparagus once or twice, until completely browned and caramelized, 16 to 20 minutes. Let cool, then cut into 1-inch pieces.

Turn a large baking sheet upside down, or use a pizza peel. Dust the surface with flour. Form one piece of the dough into a 12-inch round (see page 18) and set it on the baking sheet or peel.

Working quickly, dab the dough with one-fourth of the chili paste, dispersing it so that every pizza slice will get a pop of spiciness. Scatter one-fourth each of the garlic, asparagus, and mozzarella over the dough. Drizzle with olive oil and sprinkle with one-fourth of the Grana Padano.

Jiggle the pizza gently on the pan (or peel) to make sure it is not sticking (if it is, loosen it and sprinkle a little more flour under the area where it stuck). Slide the pizza onto the hot stone, making sure to start at the stone's back end so that the entire pizza will fit on it.

Cook the pizza for 3 minutes. Turn on the broiler. Broil the pizza until golden, crisp, and a bit blistery and charred in places, 1 to 3 minutes (watch it carefully to see that it does not burn). If you don't have a peel, use tongs to slide the pizza onto a large platter. Sprinkle with a little more of the Grana Padano and one-fourth of the lemon juice. Drizzle with more olive oil and finish with a generous sprinkling of sea salt.

Repeat with the remaining dough and toppings.

Note: You can buy Calabrian chili paste in Italian specialty markets. Or sprinkle hot chili powder over each pizza instead. You're looking for a spicy bite to contrast with the sweetness of the roasted asparagus.

Garlic Scape, Olive, Basil, and Provolone Piccante Pizza

This pizza, from our former longtime chef John Adler, is a riff on a great slice of garlic bread. Garlic scapes—long and loopy pale green garlic stalks—are abundant in farmers' markets all summer long, but there's only so much you can do with them beyond turning them into a butter for crostini or pickling them for salads. Here the sweet and flavorful stalks are roasted until tender and caramelized, then cooked down in a rich tomato sauce with good olives and red onion. Combined with provolone cheese and basil, they make for a perfectly balanced, deeply flavored pizza that's ideal for the summertime. | **MAKES FOUR 12-INCH PIZZAS, SERVING 4 TO 6**

FOR THE GARLIC SCAPES

1 ¼ pounds garlic scapes, trimmed and cut into 2-inch pieces

½ cup plus 2 tablespoons extra-virgin olive oil

¼ teaspoon kosher salt, plus more to taste

¼ teaspoon (10 turns) black pepper, plus more to taste

1 cup finely chopped red onion

2 tablespoons chopped garlic

3 tablespoons tomato paste

¼ teaspoon chili flakes

3 ounces pitted Nocellara or Calabrese olives, finely chopped (about ¼ cup)

½ teaspoon red wine vinegar

3 tablespoons torn basil leaves

FOR THE PIZZA
Franny's Pizza Dough (page 13)
All-purpose flour
**5½ ounces pitted Nocellara
or Calabrese olives, halved**
(about ½ cup)
**5½ ounces Provolone piccante,
grated or coarsely ground**
(about 1 cup)

About ⅔ cup fresh basil leaves
(20 to 28 leaves)
**Extra-virgin olive oil for
drizzling**
**2 ounces Grana Padano,
finely grated** (about ½ cup)
Sea salt

To make the garlic scapes: Preheat the oven to 500°F. Arrange an oven rack in the top third of the oven and place a pizza stone on the rack. Let heat for 1 hour.

Once the oven has preheated (and while the pizza stone continues to heat), toss the scapes with 2 tablespoons of the olive oil and the salt and pepper. Spread on a large rimmed baking sheet and roast until the scapes are completely soft and limp with some dark brown spots, 10 to 15 minutes.

Meanwhile, make the soffrito: In a large skillet over medium heat, heat the ½ cup olive oil. Add the onion and garlic and cook over medium-low heat until very soft and with very little color, about 10 minutes. Stir in the tomato paste and chili flakes, increase the heat to medium-high, and cook for 2 to 3 minutes.

Stir in the roasted scapes and chopped olives, cover, and cook over low heat, until the scapes start to absorb the sauce, about 10 minutes. Remove from the heat and sprinkle with the red wine vinegar and torn basil. Season with salt and pepper to taste.

Remove the pizza dough from the refrigerator at least 30 minutes before baking.

CONTINUED

Turn a large baking sheet upside down, or use a pizza peel. Dust the surface with flour. Form one piece of the dough into a 12-inch round (see page 18) and set it on the baking sheet or peel.

Working quickly, scatter one-quarter each of the scape mixture, olives, and Provolone and 5 to 7 basil leaves, depending on their size, over the dough. Drizzle with 2 teaspoons olive oil.

Jiggle the pizza gently on the pan (or peel) to make sure it is not sticking (if it is, loosen it and sprinkle a little more flour under the area where it stuck). Slide the pizza onto the hot stone, making sure to start at the stone's back end so that the entire pizza will fit on it.

Cook the pizza for 3 minutes. Turn on the broiler. Broil the pizza until golden, crisp, and a bit blistery and charred in places, 1 to 4 minutes (watch it carefully to see that it does not burn). If you don't have a pizza peel, use tongs to slide the pizza onto a large platter. Sprinkle with one-fourth of the Grana Padano and a pinch of sea salt and drizzle with more olive oil.

Repeat with the remaining dough and toppings.

Zucchini, Buffalo Mozzarella, and Basil Pizza

On a trip to Rome, Andrew stopped to grab some lunch at Volpetti. It's his favorite food shop in Rome, with a self-service restaurant next door. It was summer, prime zucchini season, so Andrew ordered pizza topped with mozzarella, zucchini, and zucchini blossoms. Coming up with a version that worked for Franny's, though, was a struggle. Originally the zucchini slices went on raw, and when the pizza emerged from the oven, the zucchini was bland and almost watery. It was Chef Danny Amend's clever idea to roast the slices first, condensing them and developing their flavor, and then the pizza came out perfectly. When we have access to them, we add zucchini blossoms to this pizza as well—they make for a stunning presentation. | **MAKES FOUR 12-INCH PIZZAS, SERVING 4 TO 6**

FOR THE ZUCCHINI
4 medium zucchini, trimmed
2 tablespoons extra-virgin
 olive oil
¾ teaspoon kosher salt

FOR THE PIZZA
Franny's Pizza Dough (page 13)
All-purpose flour
4 small garlic cloves, shaved
 into paper-thin slices with a
 knife or a mandoline
½ teaspoon chili flakes

12 ounces fresh mozzarella,
 preferably buffalo, pulled
 into bite-sized pieces (about
 2 cups)
1 bunch basil
Scant 3 tablespoons extra-virgin
 olive oil, plus more
 for drizzling
2 ounces Parmigiano-Reggiano
 or Grana Padano, finely
 grated (about ½ cup)
Sea salt

CONTINUED

To make the zucchini: Preheat the oven to 450°F. Slice each zucchini lengthwise into ¼-inch-thick slabs. Spread them in a single layer on a rimmed baking sheet. Drizzle with the olive oil and sprinkle with the salt. Roast until just tender but not limp, 7 to 10 minutes. Cool. (You can roast the zucchini 8 hours ahead; store at room temperature.)

Increase the oven temperature to 500°F, arrange a rack in the top third of the oven, and place a pizza stone on the rack. Let heat for 1 hour. Remove the pizza dough from the refrigerator at least 30 minutes before baking.

Turn a large baking sheet upside down, or use a pizza peel. Dust the surface with flour. Form one piece of the dough into a 12-inch round (see page 18) and set it on the baking sheet or peel.

Working quickly, scatter the dough with one-fourth of the garlic and a generous pinch of chili flakes. Arrange one-fourth of the zucchini slices on top of the pizza. Scatter one-fourth of the mozzarella and 5 to 7 basil leaves, depending on their size, over the zucchini. Drizzle with 2 teaspoons of the olive oil.

Jiggle the pizza gently on the pan (or peel) to make sure it is not sticking (if it is, loosen it and sprinkle a little more flour under the area where it stuck). Slide the pizza onto the hot stone, making sure to start at the stone's back end so that the entire pizza will fit on it.

Cook the pizza for 3 minutes. Turn on the broiler. Broil the pizza until golden, crisp, and a bit blistery and charred in places, 2 to 4 minutes (watch it carefully to see that it does not burn). If you don't have a peel, use tongs to slide the pizza onto a large platter. Sprinkle with one-fourth of the Parmigiano-Reggiano and a pinch of sea salt, and drizzle with more olive oil.

Repeat with the remaining dough and toppings.

Ricotta, Buffalo Mozzarella, Oregano, and Cherry Tomato Pizza

The classic Neapolitan *pizza filetti* studded with fresh cherry tomatoes was the inspiration for this pizza. But instead of scattering raw cherry tomatoes over the dough, we slow-roast them first. If you want to make a big batch, they will hold, submerged in olive oil and stored in the fridge, for at least a couple of weeks. They're delicious on everything: salad, pasta, even scrambled eggs. And on this pizza the little bursts of tart-sweet concentrated tomato flavor are just terrific paired with the creamy ricotta and buffalo mozzarella. | **MAKES FOUR 12-INCH PIZZAS, SERVING 4 TO 6**

FOR THE TOMATOES
2 cups cherry tomatoes, halved
2 teaspoons extra-virgin olive oil, plus more to taste
¼ teaspoon kosher salt
Pinch of freshly cracked black pepper

FOR THE PIZZA
Franny's Pizza Dough (page 13)
All-purpose flour
5 ounces (½ cup) **fresh ricotta**

12 ounces fresh mozzarella, preferably buffalo, pulled into bite-sized pieces (about 2 cups)
1 large bunch basil
2 tablespoons extra-virgin olive oil, plus more for drizzling
2 ounces Parmigiano-Reggiano or Grana Padano, finely grated (about ½ cup)
Sea salt

To roast the tomatoes: Preheat the oven to 225°F. Arrange the tomatoes cut side up on a rimmed baking sheet. Drizzle with the olive oil and season with the salt and pepper. Roast until the tomatoes have lost 50 percent of their volume, 1½ to 2 hours. Cool.

CONTINUED

Transfer the tomatoes to a container and cover with olive oil. (They will keep in the fridge for 2 weeks.)

When you are ready to bake the pizzas, preheat the oven to 500°F, with a pizza stone on a rack in the top third of the oven. Let heat for 1 hour. Remove the pizza dough from the refrigerator at least 30 minutes before baking.

Turn a large baking sheet upside down, or use a pizza peel. Dust the surface with flour. Form one piece of the dough into a 12-inch round (see page 18) and set it on the baking sheet or peel.

Working quickly, dot the dough with one-fourth of the ricotta, followed by one-fourth of the mozzarella. Scatter 5 to 7 basil leaves (depending on their size) over the pizza and drizzle with 1½ teaspoons of the olive oil.

Jiggle the pizza gently on the pan (or peel) to make sure it is not sticking (if it is, loosen it and sprinkle a little more flour under the area where it stuck). Slide the pizza onto the hot stone, making sure to start at the stone's back end so that the entire pizza will fit on it.

Cook the pizza for 3 minutes. Turn on the broiler. Broil the pizza until golden, crisp, and a bit blistery and charred in places, 2 to 4 minutes (watch it carefully to see that it does not burn). If you don't have a peel, use tongs to slide the pizza onto a large platter.

Top the pizza with one-fourth of the tomatoes (about 12) and 1 tablespoon of the tomato oil. Sprinkle with one-fourth of the Parmigiano-Reggiano and a pinch of sea salt and drizzle with additional olive oil.

Repeat with the remaining dough and toppings.

Tomato, Eggplant, Chili, Caper, and Mozzarella Pizza

Wood-roasted Japanese eggplant is one of our favorite things to eat in summer. Here we marinate it with the oil from our homemade garlic confit and use it as a pizza topping along with capers and tangy mozzarella. Eggplant has a natural bitterness that is countered by the sweet aromatic notes of the oil. Those sweet, garlicky flavors go particularly well with the char on the eggplant, which also makes it a little smoky. | **MAKES FOUR 12-INCH PIZZAS, SERVING 4 TO 6**

1¾ pounds Japanese eggplant, sliced into ¼-inch-thick rounds

1½ teaspoons kosher salt

½ cup extra-virgin olive oil, plus more for drizzling

3½ tablespoons oil from Garlic Confit (recipe follows)

Franny's Pizza Dough (page 13)

All-purpose flour

1 cup Franny's Pizza Sauce (page 15)

3 tablespoons brine-packed capers, drained

12 ounces mozzarella, pulled into bite-sized pieces (about 2 cups)

Chili flakes, such as chile de árbol

2 ounces Grana Padano, finely grated (about ½ cup)

Sea salt

Arrange the eggplant in a single layer on three or four large baking sheets, leaving space between the slices. Sprinkle with the salt and let stand at room temperature for 30 minutes, or cover and refrigerate for up to 12 hours.

CONTINUED

Preheat the oven to 450°F. Squeeze out as much excess liquid from the eggplant as possible, or pat very dry. In a large bowl, toss the eggplant with the olive oil. Return the slices to the baking sheets and roast until caramelized, 10 to 15 minutes (roast them in batches if they don't all fit in your oven at once). Transfer the eggplant to a bowl and toss with the garlic oil. (The eggplant can be refrigerated for up to 1 week.)

Preheat the oven to 500°F, with a pizza stone on a rack in the top third of the oven. Let heat for 1 hour. Remove the pizza dough from the refrigerator at least 30 minutes before baking.

Turn a large baking sheet upside down, or use a pizza peel. Dust the surface with flour. Form one piece of the dough into a 12-inch round (see page 18) and set it on the baking sheet or peel.

Working quickly, spoon one-fourth of the tomato sauce over the dough. Top with one-fourth each of the capers, eggplant, and mozzarella. Sprinkle with a pinch of chili flakes.

Jiggle the pizza gently on the pan (or peel) to make sure it is not sticking (if it is, loosen it and sprinkle a little more flour under the area where it stuck). Slide the pizza onto the hot stone, making sure to start at the stone's back end so that the entire pizza will fit on it.

Cook the pizza for 3 minutes. Turn on the broiler. Broil the pizza until golden, crisp, and a bit blistery and charred in places, 2 to 4 minutes (watch it carefully to see that it does not burn). If you don't have a peel, use tongs to slide the pizza onto a large platter. Sprinkle with one-fourth of the Grana Padano, drizzle with olive oil, and finish with a generous sprinkling of sea salt.

Repeat with the remaining dough and toppings.

CONTINUED

Garlic Confit

MAKES ABOUT 1¼ CUPS

1 head garlic, cloves separated
and peeled

About 1 cup extra-virgin olive oil

Place the garlic cloves in a small skillet and pour in just enough
olive oil to cover them. Place the pan over low heat and cook the
garlic until tender and pale golden, 30 to 35 minutes. Let cool
completely.

Transfer the garlic and oil to a jar with a tight-fitting lid. The confit
will keep in the refrigerator for up to 2 weeks. Use it as a spread on
grilled or toasted bread, drizzled with more olive oil and sprinkled
with flaky sea salt.

Buffalo Mozzarella, Ricotta, Garlic, Oregano, and Hot Pepper Pizza

A pizza for cheese lovers, this is everything a white pizza should be. Of course, it's mostly about the cheese—with ultrafresh, high-quality ricotta and buffalo mozzarella and a salty sprinkling of Parmigiano-Reggiano, it's dairy in all its glory. Throw in grassy oregano, pungent garlic, and spicy house-pickled peppers, and you've got something really special. This pizza went through many makeovers, but it hasn't changed since we landed on this version. (Though in the summer, we do swap out the oregano for fresh basil leaves.)

There's nothing wrong with leaving the hot peppers off, but their sweet bite paired with a touch of spicy heat makes this pizza what it is. The first year that we pickled peppers, we bought about two hundred pounds of summer-ripe Hungarian hots. We ran out of them by the following January. Come August, our chefs, Danny Amend and John Adler, were determined to make enough to last year-round. Five hundred pounds turned out to be enough. If you're someone who enjoys things spicy, pickle more peppers than you think you'll need. They're that good. | **MAKES FOUR 12-INCH PIZZAS, SERVING 4 TO 6**

CONTINUED

Franny's Pizza Dough (page 13)

All-purpose flour

4 small garlic cloves, shaved into paper-thin slices

12 ounces fresh mozzarella, preferably buffalo, pulled into bite-sized pieces (about 2 cups)

5 ounces (about ½ cup) **fresh ricotta**

4 to 6 teaspoons minced Pickled Hot Peppers (recipe follows), **to taste**

4 pinches dried oregano or 1 bunch basil

¼ cup extra-virgin olive oil, plus more for drizzling

Sea salt

2 ounces Parmigiano-Reggiano, finely grated (about ½ cup)

Preheat the oven to 500°F, with a pizza stone on a rack in the top third of the oven. Let heat for 1 hour. Remove the pizza dough from the refrigerator at least 30 minutes before baking.

Turn a large baking sheet upside down, or use a pizza peel. Dust the surface with flour. Form one piece of the dough into a 12-inch round (see page 18) and set it on the baking sheet or peel.

Working quickly, scatter the dough with one-fourth of the garlic, followed by one-fourth of the mozzarella. Dot one-fourth of the ricotta over the top, followed by one-fourth of the hot peppers. Sprinkle with a pinch of oregano (or 7 to 10 basil leaves). Drizzle with 1 tablespoon of the olive oil and sprinkle with a pinch of salt.

Jiggle the pizza gently on the pan (or peel) to make sure it is not sticking (if it is, loosen it and sprinkle a little more flour under the area where it stuck). Slide the pizza onto the hot stone, making sure to start at the stone's back end so that the entire pizza will fit on it.

Cook the pizza for 3 minutes. Turn on the broiler. Broil the pizza until golden, crisp, and a bit blistery and charred in places, 2 to 4 minutes (watch it carefully to see that it does not burn). If you don't have a peel, use tongs to slide the pizza onto a large platter.

CONTINUED

Sprinkle with one-fourth of the Parmigiano-Reggiano, drizzle with additional olive oil, and sprinkle with salt.

Repeat with the remaining dough and toppings.

Pickled Hot Peppers

MAKES ABOUT 1 CUP

8 ounces mixed hot peppers, such as Hungarian hot wax, Anaheim, cayenne, jalapeño, serrano, cherry, and/or banana peppers, cored and seeded

1 cup white wine vinegar

½ cup moscato vinegar (see Resources, page 92)

¼ cup sugar

1 tablespoon kosher salt

1 ounce small hot peppers, such as habanero, Scotch bonnet, Granada, ghost, Brazilian bird, or Thai bird, seeded

In a medium saucepan, combine the peppers, vinegars, sugar, and salt and bring to a simmer.

Place the small hot peppers in a bowl. Pour the hot mixture over the peppers. Cool to room temperature, then transfer to an airtight container and refrigerate for 1 week.

Remove the peppers and finely chop, then return them to their pickling brine. The peppers will keep, tightly covered, in the refrigerator for 6 months or longer.

Note: Our house-pickled hot peppers are fantastic with this pizza, but you can also use store-bought pickled hot peppers, chopped.

Fontina, Pickled Hot Pepper, Caper, Pecorino Romano, and Arugula Pizza

When we moved from the old Franny's into our new space in 2013, we gained a much larger kitchen, which gave us more room to experiment with pizza. One of the ways we did this was to start a tradition of Pizza Madness, an homage to March Madness, college basketball's annual tournament. It's a fun way to engage both our cooks and our customers. The cooks get a chance to dream up new pizzas to put on the menu, and the customers get to vote for their favorites, until we get to a winner at the end of the month.

The first year of the contest, I did a parsley pesto pizza, which lost in round one. The next year, I came up with the idea for a pickled hot wax pepper and Fontina pizza, topped with arugula just before serving. Then Andrew stepped in and made it even better, adding capers. The pizza still lost in the first round. Even so, it's remained a favorite of both staff and customers alike. | **MAKES FOUR 12-INCH PIZZAS, SERVING 4 TO 6**

Franny's Pizza Dough (page 13)
All-purpose flour
4¼ ounces pickled hot peppers (see opposite and Note), **chopped** (about 1⅓ cups)
3 tablespoons brine-packed capers, drained
5 ounces Fontina cheese, finely grated (about 1⅓ cups)

2 tablespoons extra-virgin olive oil, plus more for drizzling
3½ ounces (about 4½ cups) **wild or baby arugula**
Juice of 2 lemons
Kosher salt
2 ounces Pecorino Romano, finely grated (about ½ cup)
Sea salt

CONTINUED

Preheat the oven to 500°F, with a pizza stone on a rack in the top third of the oven. Let heat for 1 hour. Remove the pizza dough from the refrigerator at least 30 minutes before baking.

Turn a large baking sheet upside down, or use a pizza peel. Dust the surface with flour. Form one piece of the dough into a 12-inch round (see page 18) and set it on the baking sheet or peel.

Working quickly, scatter one-fourth each of the peppers, capers, and Fontina over the dough. Drizzle with olive oil.

Jiggle the pizza gently on the pan (or peel) to make sure it is not sticking (if it is, loosen it and sprinkle a little more flour under the area where it stuck). Slide the pizza onto the hot stone, making sure to start at the stone's back end so that the entire pizza will fit on it.

Cook the pizza for 3 minutes. Turn on the broiler. Broil the pizza until golden, crisp, and a bit blistery and charred in places, 2 to 4 minutes (watch it carefully to see that it does not burn).

While the pizza bakes, in a large bowl, toss together the arugula, lemon juice, the 2 tablespoons olive oil, and salt to taste.

If you don't have a peel, use tongs to slide the pizza onto a large platter. Scatter one-fourth of the salad over it, then scatter one-fourth of the Pecorino over the salad, drizzle with more olive oil, and finish with a generous sprinkling of sea salt.

Repeat with the remaining dough and toppings.

Note: If you don't want to make your own pickled peppers, you can substitute jarred pickled hot cherry peppers. B&G is a widely available supermarket brand that we like.

Anchovy, Garlic, Chili, Caper, and Pecorino Pizza

Chef John Adler created this pizza, and it's one of my favorites because I lean toward pizzas without tomato sauce. They feel lighter and are more focused, flavorwise, and they almost always wind up a bit crunchier.

The key here is to chop the capers and anchovies, which makes it easier to disperse them evenly over the pizza. This ensures a great balance—you get a little bit of briny-salty goodness in each bite. Surprisingly, though this pizza is essentially smothered with anchovies, some of the most staunch anchovy haters find they enjoy them when they try this pizza. Hard lines can be drawn when it comes to anchovies, and I think that has a lot to do with people having experienced nothing but the crummy fillets on the take-out pizzas of their childhood. Bad anchovies are terrible, but good ones, such as those packed in olive oil and imported from Italy or Spain—Agostina Recca (see Resources, page 92) are fantastic—are nuanced, saline, and not at all "fishy." They are absolutely worth spending a little extra money on, and if you do, even your anchovy-averse teenager may be swayed by this delicious pizza. | **MAKES FOUR 12-INCH PIZZAS, SERVING 4 TO 6**

Franny's Pizza Dough (page 13)
All-purpose flour
16 to 24 anchovy fillets,
    depending on size, coarsely
    chopped

4 teaspoons drained capers,
    chopped
8 small garlic cloves, shaved
    into paper-thin slices
Dried oregano (see Note)

CONTINUED

Chili flakes

4 ounces Parmigiano-Reggiano, finely grated (about 1 cup)

2 ounces Pecorino Romano, finely grated (about ½ cup)

2 lemons, halved

Extra-virgin olive oil for drizzling

Preheat the oven to 500°F, with a pizza stone on a rack in the top third of the oven. Let heat for 1 hour. Remove the pizza dough from the refrigerator at least 30 minutes before baking.

Turn a large baking sheet upside down, or use a pizza peel. Dust the surface with flour. Form one piece of the dough into a 12-inch round (see page 18) and set it on the baking sheet or peel.

Working quickly, scatter the dough with one-fourth of the anchovies, capers, and garlic. Sprinkle with a pinch each of oregano and chili flakes. Scatter one-fourth of the Parmigiano-Reggiano over the pizza.

Jiggle the pizza gently on the pan (or peel) to make sure it is not sticking (if it is, loosen it and sprinkle a little more flour under the area where it stuck). Slide the pizza onto the hot stone, making sure to start at the stone's back end so that the entire pizza will fit on it.

Cook the pizza for 3 minutes. Turn on the broiler. Broil the pizza until golden, crisp, and a bit blistery and charred in places, 2 to 4 minutes (watch it carefully to see that it does not burn). If you don't have a peel, use tongs to slide the pizza onto a large platter. Scatter one-fourth of the Pecorino Romano and squeeze the juice of ½ lemon over the pizza. Finish with a drizzling of olive oil.

Repeat with the remaining dough and toppings.

Note: If you can find dried oregano imported from Sicily that's still on the stem, use it here. It has a unique, pungent flavor.

Clam, Chili, and Parsley Pizza

There's not much on the Franny's menu that reflects Andrew's training in classic French cuisine, with the prominent exception of our clam pizza. You wouldn't necessarily think so, as clam pizza is an Italian-American staple, especially in New Haven. But ours is significantly different. Andrew steams sweet littleneck clams with onions, garlic, and wine, then simmers the clam broth with a little heavy cream. This intense shellfish glaze gets painted on the dough, adding a depth of clam flavor that you don't get in the usual clam pizza. Plus, the cream sauce bubbles and caramelizes in the oven, adding even more complexity and a richness that we cut with a touch of chili and a generous handful of fresh parsley.

It's a magical combination that developed a following as soon as we put it on the menu. Former *New York Times* restaurant critic Frank Bruni waxed poetic about this pizza, and it was so popular back in the early days of the restaurant that if we had a busy night, we'd sometimes run out. And when that happened, a few folks would be truly heartbroken.

You'll notice that the clam pizza is a bit more labor-intensive than the other pizzas, but none of the steps is hard. And the results are so worth it. | **MAKES FOUR 12-INCH PIZZAS, SERVING 4 TO 6**

CONTINUED

Franny's Pizza Dough (page 13)

¼ cup extra-virgin olive oil, plus
more for drizzling

½ Spanish onion, cut
into chunks

4 garlic cloves, smashed
and peeled

1¼ cups dry white wine

4½ dozen littleneck clams
(about 6 pounds), scrubbed well

1½ cups heavy cream

All-purpose flour

Chili flakes

½ cup chopped parsley

Preheat the oven to 500°F, with a pizza stone on a rack in the top third of the oven. Let heat for 1 hour. Remove the pizza dough from the refrigerator at least 30 minutes before baking.

While the oven heats, place ¼ cup olive oil in a large pot over medium heat. Add the onion and sauté until it is limp, about 5 minutes. Add the garlic, reduce the heat to low, and cook for 7 minutes, until the edges are golden. Add the wine and bring to a simmer. Add the clams, cover the pot, and cook until the clams start to open, about 10 minutes. As they open, transfer them to a large bowl. When all the clams are cooked, simmer the liquid in the pot until it reduces to a thick glaze, about 10 minutes. Add the cream, bring to a simmer, and reduce by a quarter, 10 to 15 minutes longer. Strain through a fine-mesh sieve into a bowl and set aside. It thickens as it cools.

Meanwhile, when the clams are cool, pluck out the meat and discard the shells.

Turn a large baking sheet upside down, or use a pizza peel. Dust the surface with flour. Form one piece of the dough into a 12-inch round (see page 18) and set it on the baking sheet or peel.

Working quickly, paint the entire surface of the pizza with one-fourth of the glaze. Scatter the clams over the pizza and sprinkle with chili flakes.

CONTINUED

Jiggle the pizza gently on the pan (or peel) to make sure it is not sticking (if it is, loosen it and sprinkle a little more flour under the area where it stuck). Slide the pizza onto the hot stone, making sure to start at the stone's back end so that the entire pizza will fit on it.

Cook the pizza for 3 minutes. Turn on the broiler. Broil the pizza until golden, crisp, and a bit blistery and charred in places, 2 to 4 minutes (watch it carefully to see that it does not burn). If you don't have a peel, use tongs to slide the pizza onto a large platter. Drizzle with olive oil and scatter with one-fourth of the parsley.

Repeat with the remaining dough and toppings.

Note: Finish this pizza with a squeeze of lemon juice. It adds a bright note of acidity that helps cut the richness of the cream.

Tomato, Buffalo Mozzarella, and Basil Pizza

Without a doubt, this is the most classic, the most revered, and the most truly Neapolitan pizza on our menu. It is also Andrew's year-round favorite, even though the basil comes and goes with the change of the seasons. For most Americans, this is what they think of when they think of artisanal pizza—a perfect balance of bright-flavored tomato sauce; creamy, tangy mozzarella (we use buffalo mozzarella); and fragrant basil leaves, all on a charred and puffed crust. We like to add a finish of grated Parmigiano-Reggiano and very good olive oil, which isn't something you really see done in Naples. But it's a delicious crowning touch, and we stand by the unorthodoxy. | **MAKES FOUR 12-INCH PIZZAS, SERVING 4 TO 6**

Franny's Pizza Dough (page 13)
All-purpose flour
¾ **cup Franny's Pizza Sauce**
  (page 15)
12 ounces buffalo mozzarella,
  pulled into bite-sized pieces
  (about 2 cups)

1 bunch basil
2 ounces Parmigiano-Reggiano
  or Grana Padano, finely
  grated (about ½ cup)
Sea salt
Extra-virgin olive oil
  for drizzling

Preheat the oven to 500°F, with a pizza stone on a rack in the top third of the oven. Let heat for 1 hour. Remove the pizza dough from the refrigerator at least 30 minutes before baking.

CONTINUED

Turn a large baking sheet upside down, or use a pizza peel. Dust the surface with flour. Form one piece of the dough into a 12-inch round (see page 18) and set it on the baking sheet or peel.

Working quickly, spread one-fourth of the tomato sauce over the dough, then scatter one-fourth of the mozzarella over the pizza. Top with 5 to 7 basil leaves, depending on their size.

Jiggle the pizza gently on the pan (or peel) to make sure it is not sticking (if it is, loosen it and sprinkle a little more flour under the area where it stuck). Slide the pizza onto the hot stone, making sure to start at the stone's back end so that the entire pizza will fit on it.

Cook the pizza for 3 minutes. Turn on the broiler. Broil the pizza until golden, crisp, and a bit blistery and charred in places, 2 to 4 minutes (watch it carefully to see that it does not burn). If you don't have a peel, use tongs to slide the pizza onto a large platter. Sprinkle with one-fourth of the Parmigiano-Reggiano and a pinch of sea salt and drizzle with one-fourth of the olive oil.

Repeat with the remaining dough and toppings.

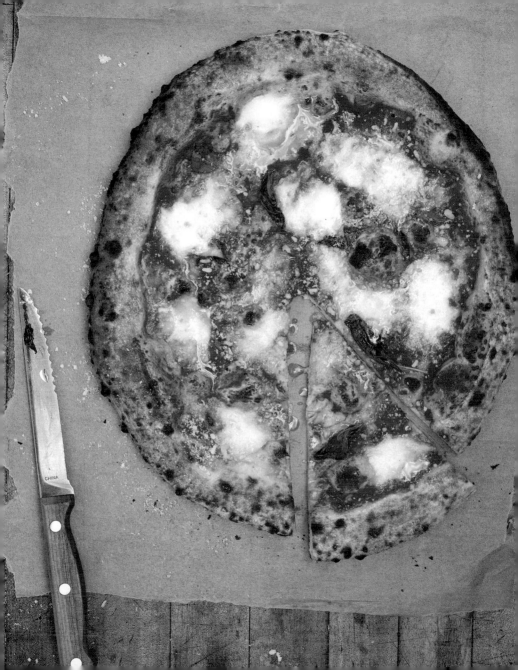

Tomato, Provolone Piccante, and Roasted Onion Pizza

There is nothing traditional about this pizza. We came up with it as a way to use provolone piccante—a wonderfully funky aged cow's-milk cheese that melts beautifully—on one of our pizzas. Provolone piccante is perfect with roasted onions—big, juicy rings that provide a honeyed contrast to the piquant aged cheese. When this pizza emerges from our oven, people whip their heads around, wondering where the incredible smell is coming from. And it's a great option for vegetarians who are craving something hearty. | **MAKES FOUR 12-INCH PIZZAS, SERVING 4 TO 6**

FOR THE ROASTED ONIONS
1 medium onion
2 tablespoons extra-virgin olive oil
¼ teaspoon kosher salt
Pinch of freshly cracked black pepper

FOR THE PIZZA
Franny's Pizza Dough (page 13)
All-purpose flour
¾ cup Franny's Pizza Sauce (page 15)

Dried oregano, preferably Sicilian (see Note, page 50)
4 ounces Calabrese olives, pitted and torn in half (about 1 cup)
5½ ounces Provolone piccante cheese, coarsely grated (about 1 cup; see Notes)
2 ounces Parmigiano-Reggiano, finely grated (about ½ cup)
Extra-virgin olive oil for drizzling

To roast the onions: Preheat the oven to 475°F. Cut the onion into ¾-inch-thick slices. Transfer the slices to a baking sheet, keeping them as intact as possible. Drizzle with the olive oil and season with the salt and pepper.

CONTINUED

Roast the onions until brown and singed on the edges, 20 to 30 minutes. Cool completely, then separate into rings. You can use the onions as soon as they are cool or store in the refrigerator for up to 5 days.

When you are ready to bake the pizza, preheat the oven to 500°F, with a pizza stone on a rack in the top third of the oven. Let heat for 1 hour. Remove the pizza dough from the refrigerator at least 30 minutes before baking.

Turn a large baking sheet upside down, or use a pizza peel. Dust the surface with flour. Form one piece of the dough into a 12-inch round (see page 18) and set it on the baking sheet or peel.

Working quickly, spread one-fourth of the tomato sauce over the dough. Sprinkle with oregano. Scatter one-fourth of the onion rings over the sauce, and then one-fourth of the olives. Scatter one-fourth of the provolone over the pizza.

Jiggle the pizza gently on the pan (or peel) to make sure it is not sticking (if it is, loosen it and sprinkle a little more flour under the area where it stuck). Slide the pizza onto the hot stone, making sure to start at the stone's back end so that the entire pizza will fit on it.

Cook the pizza for 3 minutes. Turn on the broiler. Broil the pizza until golden, crisp, and a bit charred in places, 2 to 4 minutes (watch it carefully to see that it does not burn). If you don't have a peel, use tongs to slide the pizza onto a large platter. Sprinkle with one-fourth of the Parmigiano-Reggiano and a pinch of sea salt and drizzle with olive oil.

Repeat with the remaining dough and toppings.

Notes: To get the proper grind for this cheese, cut it into 1-inch pieces and grind in a food processor until it resembles bread crumbs.

If you can't get provolone piccante, substitute caciocavallo.

Tomato, Mozzarella, and Sausage Pizza

Many people (mostly parents or their young children) come into Franny's asking for a pizza with pepperoni. We've never gone the pepperoni route, but our homemade sausage, sliced into thin rounds that sizzle in the oven, satisfies most folks' need for a spicy pork product gilding their pizza. This pizza is a big hit with kids, including ours. When our daughter, Prue, was little, we'd have the kitchen roast up a plate of the sausage and watch her demolish it. Now when a sausage pizza hits our table, our son, Marco, goes right to work, picking the slices off one by one. | **MAKES FOUR 12-INCH PIZZAS, SERVING 4 TO 6**

Franny's Pizza Dough (page 13)
All-purpose flour
¾ cup Franny's Pizza Sauce
(page 15)
5 ounces fresh mozzarella,
preferably buffalo, pulled
into bite-sized pieces
(about ¾ cup)

10 ounces Fennel Sausage
(recipe follows)**, cut into**
¼-inch-thick rounds
2 ounces Parmigiano-Reggiano
or Grana Padano, finely
grated (about ½ cup)
Sea salt
2 tablespoons extra-virgin
olive oil

Preheat the oven to 500°F, with a pizza stone on a rack in the top third of the oven. Let heat for 1 hour. Remove the pizza dough from the refrigerator at least 30 minutes before baking.

Turn a large baking sheet upside down, or use a pizza peel. Dust the surface with flour. Form one piece of the dough into a 12-inch round (see page 18) and set it on the baking sheet or peel.

CONTINUED

Working quickly, spread one-fourth of the tomato sauce over the dough. Scatter one-fourth of the mozzarella and one-fourth of the sausage over the sauce.

Jiggle the pizza gently on the pan (or peel) to make sure it is not sticking (if it is, loosen it and sprinkle a little more flour under the area where it stuck). Slide the pizza onto the hot stone, making sure to start at the stone's back end so that the entire pizza will fit on it.

Cook the pizza for 3 minutes. Turn on the broiler. Broil the pizza until golden, crisp, and a bit blistery and charred in places, 2 to 4 minutes (watch it carefully to see that it does not burn). If you don't have a peel, use tongs to slide the pizza onto a large platter. Sprinkle with one-fourth of the Parmigiano-Reggiano and a pinch of sea salt and drizzle with olive oil.

Repeat with the remaining dough and toppings.

Note: You can substitute store-bought sausage for the homemade; just be sure to seek out a good, sweet Italian variety. Cook it first before slicing and adding to the pizza.

Fennel Sausage

This adds a spicy intensity to the cheese and sweet tomato sauce of the Tomato, Mozzarella, and Sausage Pizza. Made with plenty of garlic, cracked pepper, and red chili, along with the fennel, it's more heavily seasoned than our other sausages. Pan-seared and served hot, it's excellent with soft polenta. Or tuck it into toasted rolls, with some roasted sweet peppers and onions, for a classic sandwich. Wherever you use it, fennel sausage will lend loads of deeply spiced porky flavor. | **MAKES ABOUT TEN 6-INCH LINKS (ABOUT 3 POUNDS)**

CONTINUED

FOR THE SAUSAGES

2 pounds, 10 ounces ground
pork shoulder, chilled

6 ounces ground pork belly,
chilled

2 tablespoons kosher salt

1 tablespoon finely chopped
garlic

2 teaspoons freshly cracked
black pepper

1½ teaspoons fennel seeds

½ teaspoon chili flakes

¼ cup ice water

Natural hog casings
(see Resources, page 92),
soaked and flushed
(see page 66)

2 tablespoons extra-virgin
olive oil

To make the sausages: In a large bowl, combine all the ingredients.
Using your hands (wear gloves, if you like), fold and mix together
until all the ingredients are well distributed and the meat and fat
bind together. When the mixture becomes noticeably stiff and
sticky and starts to leave a greasy film on the sides of the bowl,
stop mixing. Undermixing can lead to a dry, crumbly texture and
overmixing can lead to tough, rubbery sausages, so you want to
make sure the meat is properly mixed.

Slide the entire length of one casing onto the stuffer tube of the
sausage maker. Tie a knot in the end of the casing or secure tightly
with kitchen twine. (See Sausage Techniques, pages 66–67.) Use a
sausage pricker, a pushpin, or a thin needle to poke a few holes in
the end of the casing.

With the motor running at medium speed, use one hand to slowly
feed the ground meat mixture into the hopper of your sausage
maker and the other hand to help guide the meat as it fills the
casing. Do not work too quickly, or the casing will overfill and burst.
The sausage should feel plump and firm but have a small amount
of space to allow for expansion during cooking. When you near
the last 3 inches of casing, stop feeding the hopper with meat and
remove the sausage from the stuffing tube.

Place the sausage on a large work surface. Tie it tightly with kitchen twine at 6-inch intervals to form individual links. Trim any loose ends of twine. Knot the open end of the casing securely. Using the sausage pricker, pushpin, or needle, prick the sausage casing all over to release air bubbles. (The sausages can be refrigerated, well wrapped, for up to 5 days.)

To cook the sausages: Preheat the oven to 400°F. Cut the sausages into links and lightly oil them. Heat an ovenproof skillet over high heat. Add as many sausages as fit comfortably in the pan and sear until well browned on both sides, about 2 minutes per side. Transfer to the oven and roast until cooked through, about 8 minutes. (If using for pizza, let cool before slicing.)

Sausage Techniques

1. Hog casings are sold dried and salted, and you can find them online (see Resources, page 92). Before making sausages, you need to soak the casings to make them soft and pliable, then flush them with cold water to make sure they are completely rinsed of all residual salt.

2. Unravel the casings and soak them in a large bowl of cool water for 1 hour. Take one casing and fit one end snugly over the faucet in your kitchen sink. Run cool water through the casing for a minute or so to flush it. Transfer the casing to a small bowl of cool water to keep it moist; let one end of the casing hang over the edge of the bowl so that you can easily find it when it's time to stuff. Repeat with the remaining casings.

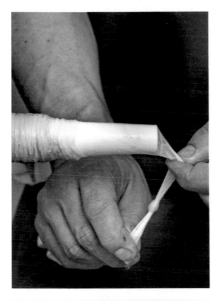

3. If the casings have dried out at all, dip them in water; they need to be well lubricated to easily slide onto the stuffer. Slide the entire length of a casing onto the sausage stuffer, bunching it up and pushing it forward as you go. Then tie a knot at the end.

4. Leave at least 3 inches of unstuffed casing to allow for expansion during tying. Tie the sausage tightly with kitchen twine at 6-inch intervals to form individual links, then tie the open end.

Tomato, Mozzarella, and Meatball Pizza

We had a meatball pizza on the menu when we first opened. This was back in the days when Andrew was making everything himself, and after a few months of rolling meatball after meatball, he got sick to death of them. And he was tired of watching the meatballs roll off the pizzas and into the wood fire, which is actually pretty funny if you're not standing in front of a pizza oven for ten hours at a time. So the pizza came off the menu (other items met that same fate; when Andrew got tired of making something, it got nixed, which left me with the unenviable task of explaining this to customers).

Once we had more experience and a well-oiled kitchen staff in place, we brought the meatball pizza back. This time around, the kitchen had the great idea of making the meatballs much larger, roasting them, and then slicing them into wedges, thus solving two problems—the kitchen crew doesn't have to make as many meatballs, and the wedges don't roll off into the fire.

These meatballs are outrageously delicious, and while they're great on the pizza, they'd be tasty elsewhere too—in sliders or on top of spaghetti. | **MAKES FOUR 12-INCH PIZZAS, SERVING 4 TO 6**

Franny's Pizza Dough (page 13)
All-purpose flour
¾ **cup Franny's Pizza Sauce**
  (page 15)
5 ounces fresh mozzarella,
  preferably buffalo, pulled
  into bite-sized pieces
  (about 1¼ cups)

12 Meatballs (recipe follows),
  cut into quarters
2 ounces Parmigiano-Reggiano,
  finely grated (about ½ cup)
2 tablespoons extra-virgin
  olive oil
Sea salt

CONTINUED

Preheat the oven to 500°F, with a pizza stone on a rack in the top third of the oven. Let heat for 1 hour. Remove the pizza dough from the refrigerator at least 30 minutes before baking.

Turn a large baking sheet upside down, or use a pizza peel. Dust the surface with flour. Form one piece of the dough into a 12-inch round (see page 18) and set it on the baking sheet or peel.

Working quickly, spread one-fourth of the tomato sauce over the dough. Scatter one-fourth of the mozzarella and one-fourth of the meatballs over the sauce.

Jiggle the pizza gently on the pan (or peel) to make sure it is not sticking (if it is, loosen it and sprinkle a little more flour under the area where it stuck). Slide the pizza onto the hot stone, making sure to start at the stone's back end so that the entire pizza will fit on it.

Cook the pizza for 3 minutes. Turn on the broiler. Broil the pizza until golden, crisp, and a bit blistery and charred in places, 2 to 4 minutes (watch it carefully to see that it does not burn). If you don't have a peel, use tongs to slide the pizza onto a large platter. Sprinkle with one-fourth of the Parmigiano-Reggiano and a pinch of sea salt and drizzle with 1½ teaspoons of the olive oil.

Repeat with the remaining dough and toppings.

Meatballs

The key component of these light, super-flavorful meatballs is the bread. Instead of using dry bread crumbs (which pull moisture from the meat itself), we soak a cubed country-style loaf in milk to make crumbs that contribute some dairy flavor and soft texture. With the moisture and binding power of the milk-soaked bread, there's no need to add eggs. The rich pork, sweet veal, and earthy beef all get their due, and they are brightened by fresh lemon zest and sharp cheese; these are spectacular meatballs. They are also relatively easy to make, because instead of frying them, you simply pop a baking sheet of meatballs into a very hot oven and roast them until they're crisp and brown all over. You may find yourself devouring them straight from the pan. | **MAKES 4 TO 4½ DOZEN MEATBALLS**

6 ounces day-old country-style
  bread, crust removed
¾ cup whole milk
1 pound ground beef, chilled
1 pound ground veal, chilled
1 pound ground pork, chilled
1 cup finely chopped onion
2 ounces Parmigiano-Reggiano,
  finely grated (about ½ cup)

½ cup chopped flat-leaf parsley
3 garlic cloves, minced
2 tablespoons kosher salt
2¼ teaspoons freshly cracked
  black pepper
Finely grated zest of 1 lemon
Extra-virgin olive oil

Preheat the oven to 500°F. Cut the bread into ½-inch cubes and place in a bowl. You should have about 4 cups. Pour the milk over and let stand until the bread has absorbed most of the liquid.

CONTINUED

In a large bowl, gently fold together the beef, veal, pork, onion, bread, cheese, parsley, garlic, salt, pepper, and lemon zest. Mix only until just combined (see Note)—keep the mixture as loose as possible.

Roll the meat into Ping Pong–sized balls and place at least an inch apart on two large rimmed baking sheets. It's easiest to shape very cold meat, so if the mixture warms up, chill it again until cold. Brush the meatballs generously with olive oil.

Roast the meatballs, turning several times, until golden and cooked through, about 10 minutes.

Note: As you're mixing your meats, bread, and seasonings together, be thorough but gentle. If you're too aggressive and you overmix, your meatballs could end up a little tough. Mix just enough to evenly distribute the ingredients, no more.

Prosciutto Cotto, Caciocavallo, and Roasted Pepper Pizza

I think our chefs, Danny Amend and John Adler, created this pizza because they wanted an excuse to make their own ham at the restaurant. If that's something you also want to try at home, by all means, make our prosciutto cotto. But if not, a good store-bought ham will work just fine. Some of our guests call this the "ham and cheese pizza," and while I wouldn't want to call it that on our menu, it's a fairly accurate description— though with the addition of silky roasted peppers, it's a pretty elegant ham and cheese. Some of the pieces of ham curl up around the edges, getting all crispy and irresistible. And the caciocavallo lends a delicious creamy tanginess next to the soft, sweet peppers. | **MAKES FOUR 12-INCH PIZZAS, SERVING 4 TO 6**

1 large red bell pepper
Franny's Pizza Dough
  (page 13)
All-purpose flour
6 ounces caciocavallo,
  finely grated
  (about 1½ cups)

12 ounces prosciutto cotto,
  homemade (recipe follows),
  or other good-quality sliced
  baked ham, torn into bite-
  sized pieces
1 small onion, sliced into thin
  rings
Sea salt
2 ounces Parmigiano-Reggiano,
  finely grated (about ½ cup)
¼ cup extra-virgin olive oil

Preheat the oven to 500°F, with a pizza stone on a rack in the top third of the oven. Let heat for 1 hour. Remove the pizza dough from the refrigerator at least 30 minutes before baking.

CONTINUED

Meanwhile, place the pepper over a high flame on the stovetop and char the pepper, turning it occasionally, until it is blackened all over but not falling apart. (If you don't have a gas stove, broil the pepper beforehand instead.) Place the pepper in a deep bowl, cover with aluminum foil, and let stand for 10 minutes. Using your fingers or a paring knife, scrape off the blackened skin. Remove and discard the seeds and cut the pepper into 1/4-inch-wide strips.

Turn a large baking sheet upside down, or use a pizza peel. Dust the surface with flour. Form one piece of the dough into a 12-inch round (see page 18) and set it on the baking sheet or peel.

Working quickly, scatter the dough with one-fourth of the caciocavallo, followed by one-fourth of the ham, one-fourth of the onion, and a pinch of sea salt.

Jiggle the pizza gently on the pan (or peel) to make sure it is not sticking (if it is, loosen it and sprinkle a little more flour under the area where it stuck). Slide the pizza onto the hot stone, making sure to start at the stone's back end so that the entire pizza will fit on it.

Cook the pizza for 3 minutes. Turn on the broiler. Broil the pizza until golden, crisp, and a bit blistery and charred in places, 2 to 4 minutes (watch it carefully to see that it does not burn). If you don't have a peel, use tongs to slide the pizza onto a large platter. Distribute one-fourth of the roasted peppers over the pizza. Sprinkle with one-fourth of the Parmigiano-Reggiano and the sea salt, and drizzle with 1 tablespoon of olive oil.

Repeat with the remaining dough and toppings.

Note: Don't use regular prosciutto here—it will just dry out in the oven. A good, moist, light pink, freshly baked or boiled prosciutto cotto is what you want. Avoid deli ham, which is filled with preservatives.

CONTINUED

Ham (Prosciutto Cotto)

Traditional *prosciutto cotto* (cooked ham) starts its life as a whole pig leg. At Franny's, we butcher the leg ourselves, but at home, it's easier to buy a 7-pound boned, skinned fresh ham from a butcher and proceed from there. You will need a brining needle (see Resources, page 92), but other than that, it's simply a matter of letting the meat brine for a few days before tying and roasting it. The roasted ham will keep for up to 2 weeks (or longer in the freezer), and you'll be blown away by the results. This is the ham we created for the Prosciutto Cotto, Caciocavallo, and Roasted Pepper Pizza (page 73), but it would make a great addition to an antipasti plate or an earthy vegetable or bean soup, or just slice it for the best ham sandwich you can imagine. | **MAKES 5½ TO 6 POUNDS**

FOR THE BRINE

8 cups water

393 grams (about 2½ cups) **kosher salt**

237 grams (about 1 cup plus 2 tablespoons) **sugar**

2 onions, halved

8 garlic cloves, smashed and peeled

4 bay leaves

3 dried chiles de árbol

2 teaspoons black peppercorns

36 grams Cure #1 (aka pink curing salt; see Note)

6 quarts ice water

One 7-pound piece boneless, skinless fresh ham (pork leg), **preferably ham sirloin** (fat left on)

1 bunch rosemary

1 bunch sage

To make the brine: In a large pot, combine the 8 cups water, salt, sugar, onions, garlic, bay leaves, chiles, and peppercorns. Bring to a simmer and simmer until the sugar and salt are completely dissolved and the onions are soft, about 5 minutes. Remove from the heat and stir in the pink curing salt. Cool completely. (The brine should be very cold when you add the meat.)

Pour the ice water into a receptacle large enough to hold the meat and brine. Add the cooled brine. Add the meat. Cover tightly with plastic wrap or a tight-fitting lid and refrigerate for 24 hours.

Remove the meat from the brine. Fill a brining needle with some of the brine and inject it all over the ham at 1-inch intervals, refilling the needle with more brine for each injection. The meat should feel swollen and firm and filled with brine. Return to the container of brine, cover, and refrigerate for 4 more days.

When ready to cook the ham, remove it from the refrigerator and let stand for 2 to 3 hours so it can come up to room temperature. Preheat the oven to 300°F. Remove the ham from the brine and pat it dry. Roll the ham into a uniformly shaped bundle (with the fat on the outside) and tie it all around, both crosswise and lengthwise, with butcher twine at 1½-inch intervals, tying the twine as tightly as possible. (The twine should have a net-like appearance when finished.) Stick the rosemary and sage bunches under the twine on the bottom of the ham.

Place the ham on a rack set over a roasting pan. Roast until the meat reaches an internal temperature of 115°F, about 2 hours and 15 minutes.

Increase the oven temperature to 475°F and roast until the meat reaches 135°F, about 30 minutes more; check the temperature every 15 minutes, as the timing may vary. Remove the herbs. Thinly slice to serve.

CONTINUED

Note: Sodium nitrite, also called Cure #1, Prague powder #1, InstaCure #1, or pink salt, is a preservative. You don't need much, but not only does it extend the shelf life of cured meats, it also gives them a particularly intense flavor and helps keep them from turning brown because of oxidation. You can find it at sausage-making supply stores, and it is easily purchased online (see Resources, page 92). You'll need a scale that can weigh grams for weighing the salt, because a volume measure won't be exact enough. When using curing salt it's important to use the exact amounts of meat and salt called for in order for the recipe to work properly; sodium nitrite is a potent chemical, and you need to be careful and precise.

Mushroom Pizza

While mushrooms certainly have seasons, there are so many good producers growing lovely cultivated mushrooms year-round, there's no reason not to turn to this pizza whenever you're in the mood for the savory satisfaction that can only come from mushrooms. Any variety will do—the more the merrier to yield 2¼ pounds total. Roast them through, letting the mushrooms release their liquid, condense, and take on a golden color. Then toss them with a bit of raw garlic, fresh rosemary and sage, and a splash of white wine vinegar. The touch of acid is a surprising addition here, but it contributes some nice complexity to an otherwise fairly straightforward pizza. Though straightforward isn't a bad thing when it comes to mushrooms—their earthy richness is all this pizza really needs. | **MAKES FOUR 12-INCH PIZZAS, SERVING 4 TO 6**

Franny's Pizza Dough (page 13)

FOR THE MUSHROOMS
6 ounces cremini mushrooms
6 ounces button mushrooms
6 ounces shiitake mushrooms
6 ounces trumpet mushrooms
6 ounces hen-of-the-woods
  mushrooms
6 ounces oyster mushrooms
½ cup extra-virgin olive oil
1 teaspoon kosher salt
½ teaspoon freshly cracked
  black pepper

1 teaspoon finely chopped
  rosemary
1 teaspoon finely chopped sage
1 teaspoon finely chopped
  garlic
1 tablespoon white wine vinegar

8 ounces mozzarella, preferably
  buffalo, pulled into bite-sized
  pieces (about 1⅓ cups)
1 ounce Parmigiano-Reggiano,
  finely grated (about ¼ cup)
Sea salt
Extra-virgin olive oil for drizzling

CONTINUED

Preheat the oven to 500°F, with a pizza stone on a rack in the top third of the oven. Let heat for 1 hour. Remove the pizza dough from the refrigerator at least 30 minutes before baking.

Meanwhile, clean the mushrooms with a damp paper towel. Cut into bite-sized pieces. Divide the olive oil between two large skillets and heat over high heat until the oil begins to ripple but is not smoking. Add the cremini, button, and shiitake mushrooms to one pan; add the trumpet, hen-of-the-woods, and oyster mushrooms to the other. Cook the mushrooms for 1 minute, tossing them constantly, then reduce the heat to medium. Add half the salt and pepper to each pan and cook until the mushrooms are well caramelized, 3 to 5 minutes more. Remove from the heat and transfer the mushrooms to a large bowl. Add the herbs and toss for 30 seconds, then stir in the garlic and vinegar. Let cool.

Turn a large baking sheet upside down, or use a pizza peel. Dust the surface with flour. Form one piece of the dough into a 12-inch round (see page 18) and set it on the baking sheet or peel.

Working quickly, scatter the dough with one-fourth of the mushroom mixture and then one-fourth of the mozzarella.

Jiggle the pizza gently on the pan (or peel) to make sure it is not sticking (if it is, loosen it and sprinkle a little more flour under the area where it stuck). Slide the pizza onto the hot stone, making sure to start at the stone's back end so that the entire pizza will fit on it.

Cook the pizza for 3 minutes. Turn on the broiler. Broil the pizza until golden, crisp, and a bit blistery and charred in places, 2 to 4 minutes (watch it carefully to see that it does not burn). If you don't have a peel, use tongs to slide the pizza onto a large platter. Sprinkle with one-fourth of the Parmigiano-Reggiano and the sea salt. Finish with a drizzling of olive oil.

Repeat with the remaining dough and toppings.

Note: We make this pizza using a combination of whatever mushrooms are looking good at the moment. We group the mushrooms with similar cooking times and cook them in the same pan. You don't want to mix a short-cooking mushroom with one that needs longer to cook. Then mix all the mushrooms together with the aromatics before topping the pizzas.

Tomato, Garlic, Oregano, and Extra-Virgin Olive Oil Pizza

This is a pizza that some folks initially just didn't get. It's a cheeseless tomato-sauced pizza—but it's entirely traditional, a true Neapolitan pizza. Called *pizza marinara*, it consists of a red slick of tomato sauce, plenty of garlic and oregano, and lots of olive oil. It doesn't need any cheese—Naples knows what it's doing. And having this pizza on the menu means we've been able to offer something to vegans that they very rarely get to eat: good pizza. At home, this would make a lovely addition to a meal that perhaps featured protein elsewhere. This is definitely one of those times to pull out your very best olive oil—be liberal applying it. | **MAKES FOUR 12-INCH PIZZAS, SERVING 4 TO 6**

Franny's Pizza Dough (page 13)
All-purpose flour
1 cup Franny's Pizza Sauce
  (page 15)
12 or 13 Calabrese olives, pitted
4 small garlic cloves, shaved
  into paper-thin slices

Dried oregano, preferably
  Sicilian (see Note, page 50)
Sea salt
6 tablespoons extra-virgin
  olive oil

Preheat the oven to 500°F, with a pizza stone on a rack in the top third of the oven. Let heat for 1 hour. Remove the pizza dough from the refrigerator at least 30 minutes before baking.

Turn a large baking sheet upside down, or use a pizza peel. Dust the surface with flour. Form one piece of the dough into a 12-inch round (see page 18) and set it on the baking sheet or peel.

CONTINUED

Working quickly, spread one-fourth of the tomato sauce over the crust. Scatter one-fourth of the olives and garlic over the sauce. Sprinkle the pizza with dried oregano and a pinch of sea salt.

Jiggle the pizza gently on the pan (or peel) to make sure it is not sticking (if it is, loosen it and sprinkle a little more flour under the area where it stuck). Slide the pizza onto the hot stone, making sure to start at the stone's back end so that the entire pizza will fit on it.

Cook the pizza for 3 minutes. Turn on the broiler. Broil the pizza until golden, crisp, and a bit blistery and charred in places, 2 to 4 minutes (watch it carefully to see that it does not burn). If you don't have a peel, use tongs to slide the pizza onto a large platter. Sprinkle with sea salt and drizzle with 1½ tablespoons of the olive oil.

Repeat with the remaining dough and toppings.

Pizza Rustica

Though the Neapolitan name for this traditional recipe uses the word "pizza," it's actually a creamy tart. It's quite sturdy and therefore is good picnic fare—lovely to eat at the park or the beach. And it's a great way to use up leftover salami scraps if you have any—though the tart is so good, it's totally worth buying salami just for it. The buttery short-crust pastry, made with white wine and lemon, has a touch of sweetness, and with the savory richness of the cured meat and the milky ricotta, the result is divine. Next to a cool, crunchy salad, this would make an elegant lunch, or even brunch. | **SERVES 8 TO 10**

FOR THE CRUST

2¾ cups all-purpose flour

4 teaspoons sugar

1½ teaspoons kosher salt

Grated zest of 1 lemon

12 tablespoons (1½ sticks) **unsalted butter, cubed and chilled**

1 large egg, plus 1 egg beaten with 1 tablespoon water for an egg wash for the top

1 large egg white

2 tablespoons dry white wine

FOR THE FILLING

2 cups (1¼ pounds) **ricotta**

3 ounces Pecorino Romano cheese, finely grated (about ¾ cup)

2 large eggs

1 large egg yolk

¼ teaspoon kosher salt

8 ounces fresh mozzarella, cut into ¼-inch cubes

One 2-ounce piece salami, cut into ¼-inch cubes

One 2-ounce piece prosciutto cotto or other mild baked ham, cut into ¼-inch cubes

½ teaspoon freshly cracked black pepper

¼ teaspoon chili flakes

2 tablespoons chopped flat-leaf parsley

CONTINUED

To make the crust: In a large bowl, combine the flour, sugar, salt, and lemon zest. Toss in the butter. Cover the bowl with plastic wrap and freeze for 10 minutes.

Transfer the mixture to a food processor and pulse until it resembles coarse crumbs. Add the egg and egg white and pulse until combined. With the food processor running, add the wine and process until the dough just comes together.

Turn the dough out into a bowl and briefly knead it. Divide the dough into 2 pieces, one about 16 ounces, the other about 8 ounces. Shape each piece into a round, wrap it in plastic wrap, and refrigerate for at least 2 hours before rolling.

Preheat the oven to 325°F. On a lightly floured surface, roll the larger round of dough into a 12-inch circle. Transfer it to a 9-inch springform pan (the dough won't come all the way up the sides). Line the crust with parchment paper and fill it with dried beans or pie weights.

Bake the crust for 20 minutes. Remove the parchment and beans or weights and bake for 5 to 10 minutes longer, until the shell is golden brown. Let cool completely. Increase the oven temperature to 350°F.

To make the filling: In a food processor, combine the ricotta, Pecorino Romano, eggs, and yolk and process until smooth. Scrape the mixture into a bowl and fold in the rest of the filling ingredients. Pour the filling into the cooled tart shell.

On a lightly floured surface, roll out the smaller dough round to a 10-inch circle. Cut it into 1-inch-wide strips. Lay half the strips over the filling, spacing them about ¼ inch apart. Weave the remaining strips over and under the first strips, forming a lattice. Press the ends of the strips into the bottom crust.

Brush with the egg wash, and bake until the filling is just set, about 40 minutes. Serve warm or at room temperature.

Calzone with Braised Greens, Ricotta, and Tomato

While calzone fillings can change seasonally—we use ingredients like wild mushrooms in the fall and Sun Gold cherry tomatoes in the summer—this is the most classic rendition. The calzone is filled with creamy ricotta and sautéed greens and then topped with tomato sauce, which caramelizes around the edges when baked. It may seem odd that for this recipe we call for packaged supermarket mozzarella instead of a milky fior di latte, but the low-moisture cheese gets stretchy as it melts, which is what you want in a calzone. | **MAKES FOUR 12-INCH CALZONES, SERVING 4 TO 6**

¼ cup extra-virgin olive oil, plus
  more as needed
1 small onion, diced
2 garlic cloves, finely chopped
¾ teaspoon kosher salt, plus
  more as needed
1 bunch leafy greens
  (about 12 ounces), **such as**
  turnip tops or Tuscan kale,
  center ribs removed
17½ ounces (about 1¾ cups)
  fresh ricotta

Franny's Pizza Dough
  (page 13)
All-purpose flour
4 ounces Grana Padano,
  finely grated (about 1 cup)
3½ ounces low-moisture
  mozzarella, finely diced
  (not shredded; about 1 cup)
½ cup Franny's Pizza Sauce
  (page 15)
2 ounces Pecorino Romano,
  finely grated (about ½ cup)

Preheat the oven to 500°F, with a pizza stone on a rack in the top third of the oven. Let heat for 1 hour.

CONTINUED

In a large skillet, heat the olive oil over medium heat. Add the onion and garlic, season with a pinch of salt, and cook, stirring occasionally, until very soft but not browned, about 10 minutes.

Increase the heat to medium-high. Stir in the greens a handful at a time, letting them slightly wilt before adding more, then stir in ½ cup water and the ¾ teaspoon salt and cook the greens, tossing them occasionally, until very tender, 10 to 15 minutes. If the skillet seems dry at any point, add a few tablespoons of water to moisten the greens. Let the greens cool, then finely chop.

In a small bowl, combine the greens and ricotta. Season with salt as needed.

At least 30 minutes before baking, remove the pizza dough from the refrigerator. Place a small rimmed baking sheet on the pizza stone to preheat.

Lightly dust your work surface with flour. Using a rolling pin, roll one piece of dough into a 10-inch round.

Working quickly, spread one-fourth of the ricotta-greens mixture over half the dough round. Top with one-fourth each of the Grana Padano and mozzarella. Fold the other half of the dough over the filling, pushing out any air bubbles. Press the edges together to seal, then use a pizza wheel or paring knife to trim the excess dough from the edges.

Remove the preheated baking sheet from the oven and brush it lightly with olive oil. Transfer the calzone to the prepared pan. Spread one-fourth of the tomato sauce over the top of the calzone. Place the pan on the pizza stone and bake until the calzone is golden, 10 to 12 minutes. Turn on the broiler. Broil the calzone until the tomato sauce is well caramelized, 2 to 3 minutes. Scatter one-fourth of the Pecorino over the calzone and finish with a drizzling of olive oil.

Repeat with the remaining dough and filling.

Resources

Italian Pantry Items

Salt-packed capers from
Pantelleria, moscato vinegar,
high-quality anchovies,
excellent olive oils, and
San Marzano tomatoes

bklynlarder.com
buonitalia.com
gustiamo.com

Note: For a cheater's moscato
vinegar substitute, whisk together
1/2 cup apple cider vinegar,
2 1/2 teaspoons honey, and
1/4 teaspoon balsamic vinegar.

Dried Herbs and Spices

Lucknow fennel seeds

bklynlarder.com
kalustyans.com
madecasse.com
manicaretti.com
thespicehouse.com

Heritage Meats

heritagefoodsusa.com
nimanranch.com

Curing Supplies

Cure #1 pink salt, hog casings,
meat injection pump (aka brining
needle), and sausage stuffers

butcher-packer.com
sausagemaker.com

Flours

Premium flours, including all-
purpose

kingarthurflour.com

Index

Conversion Charts

Here are rounded-off equivalents between the metric system and the traditional systems that are used in the United States to measure weight and volume.

FRACTIONS / DECIMALS

FRACTIONS	DECIMALS
⅛	.125
¼	.25
⅓	.33
⅜	.375
½	.5
⅝	.625
⅔	.67
¾	.75
⅞	.875

WEIGHTS

US/UK	METRIC
¼ oz	7 g
½ oz	15 g
1 oz	30 g
2 oz	55 g
3 oz	85 g
4 oz	110 g
5 oz	140 g
6 oz	170 g
7 oz	200 g
8 oz (½ lb)	225 g
9 oz	250 g
10 oz	280 g
11 oz	310 g
12 oz	340 g
13 oz	370 g
14 oz	400 g
15 oz	425 g
16 oz (1 lb)	455 g

VOLUME

AMERICAN	IMPERIAL	METRIC
¼ tsp		1.25 ml
½ tsp		2.5 ml
1 tsp		5 ml
½ Tbsp (1½ tsp)		7.5 ml
1 Tbsp (3 tsp)		15 ml
¼ cup (4 Tbsp)	2 fl oz	60 ml
⅓ cup (5 Tbsp)	2½ fl oz	75 ml
½ cup (8 Tbsp)	4 fl oz	125 ml
⅔ cup (10 Tbsp)	5 fl oz	150 ml
¾ cup (12 Tbsp)	6 fl oz	175 ml
1 cup (16 Tbsp)	8 fl oz	250 ml
1¼ cups	10 fl oz	300 ml
1½ cups	12 fl oz	350 ml
2 cups (1 pint)	16 fl oz	500 ml
2½ cups	20 fl oz (1 pint)	625 ml
5 cups	40 fl oz (1 qt)	1.25 l

OVEN TEMPERATURES

	°F	°C	GAS MARK
very cool	250–275	130–140	½–1
cool	300	148	2
warm	325	163	3
moderate	350	177	4
moderately hot	375–400	190–204	5–6
hot	425	218	7
very hot	450–475	232–245	8–9

°C/F TO °F/C CONVERSION CHART

°C/F	°C	°F	°C/F	°C	°F	°C/F	°C	°F	°C/F	°C	°F
90	32	194	220	104	428	350	177	662	480	249	896
100	38	212	230	110	446	360	182	680	490	254	914
110	43	230	240	116	464	370	188	698	500	260	932
120	49	248	250	121	482	380	193	716	510	266	950
130	54	266	260	127	500	390	199	734	520	271	968
140	60	284	270	132	518	400	204	752	530	277	986
150	66	302	280	138	536	410	210	770	540	282	1,004
160	71	320	290	143	554	420	216	788	550	288	1,022
170	77	338	300	149	572	430	221	806			
180	82	356	310	154	590	440	227	824			
190	88	374	320	160	608	450	232	842			
200	93	392	330	166	626	460	238	860			
210	99	410	340	171	644	470	243	878			

Example: If your temperature is 90°F, your conversion is 32°C; if your temperature is 90°C, your conversion is 194°F.

Library of Congress Cataloging-in-Publication Data

Names: Feinberg, Andrew, 1974– author. | Stephens, Francine, author. | Clark, Melissa, author.
Title: The artisanal kitchen : perfect pizza at home / Andrew Feinberg, Francine Stephens, Melissa Clark.
Description: New York, NY : Artisan, a division of Workman Publishing Company, Inc. [2017]
Identifiers: LCCN 2016032082 | ISBN 9781579657635 (hardback, paper over board)
Subjects: LCSH: Cooking (Pizza)–Italy. | Seasonal cooking–Italy. | Cooking, Italian. | LCGFT: Cookbooks.
Classification: LCC TX770.P58 F45 2017 | DDC 641.82/48–dc23
LC record available at https://lccn.loc.gov/2016032082

Artisan books are available at special discounts when purchased in bulk for premiums and sales promotions as well as for fund-raising or educational use. Special editions or book excerpts also can be created to specification. For details, contact the Special Sales Director at the address below, or send an e-mail to specialmarkets@workman.com.

Published by Artisan
A division of Workman Publishing Co., Inc.
225 Varick Street
New York, NY 10014-4381
artisanbooks.com

Artisan is a registered trademark of Workman Publishing Co., Inc.

Portions of this book have been adapted from material that appears in *Franny's: Simple Seasonal Italian* (Artisan, 2013).

Published simultaneously in Canada by Thomas Allen & Son, Limited

Printed in China
First printing, May 2017

10 9 8 7 6 5 4 3 2 1